Teasing

Deal with it before the joke's on you

Steve Pitt • Illustrated by Remie Geoffroi

James Lorimer & Company Ltd., Publishers
Toronto

The orthodontist has finally taken off your braces,

and your smile looks like a movie star's!

But ever since you started wearing a retainer, you've been having a hard time pronouncing the letter "s." It was no big deal, until this big kid named Norman says, "Hey! He talkth like thith…"

Even you laughed—the first time. But two weeks later it's no longer funny. In fact, it's getting really annoying.

Sometimes teasing is no joke.

The word "teasing" comes from the old Anglo Saxon word *teesan*. It described how people untangled raw wool using paddles lined with sharp hooks. Today, teasing is a certain kind of humour. Poking a little fun at someone can give everyone a big laugh. But it can also make that person feel pulled apart like wool—wanting to be good-humoured, but hurting inside.

Whether or not we mean it to, humour sometimes hurts.

If you have ever been teased, you know how bad it can feel. And we've probably all accidentally hurt someone's feelings with a joke. This book can help you avoid hurting with humour, and offers suggestions for dealing with the conflicts that come up when teasing goes too far.

Contents

What is

All right, we all know what teasing is, don't we?

In the olden days it meant "to pluck," and you can kind of see the connection—to pluck your sister's hair, or to pick at someone's sore spot. Teasing is a common way to share humour with the people around you by

- playing keep-away
- sharing practical jokes
- tickling
- mimicking someone
- tantalizing someone with a secret
- tempting someone with a treat
- keeping someone guessing

Teasing?

Everyone needs a laugh now and then, right? But sometimes teasing is funnier to the teaser than the person being teased. Ever notice what can happen when you

- make fun of someone?
- put someone down?
- cruelly imitate someone?
- are annoying?
- call names?
- taunt someone?
- harass someone?
- harp on someone's habits or behaviour?
- point out someone's flaws?

Teasing can be a way of showing affection for another person. But teasing can also be used to embarrass people and hurt their feelings. Teasing that hurts is a form of bullying. And we all know that bullying is serious business.

EXCLUDE

Man, Rickie's won a medal in every event!

Ali, Tom, and Ted are getting ready for track and field when Rickie comes in.

People may tease each

MAKE A POINT

Where are you going?

To get some juice.

Could you bring me one?

Sure.

EMBARRASS

She told me no one asked her to the dance.

Oh-oh. Here comes Debbie the Drip.

We were just talking about the dance. So, who are you going with?

INTIMIDATE

Here comes that loser, Fred.

Khalil likes to poke a little fun at the new kid.

Hey, I hear Bill is mad at you.

Me? What for? I didn't do anything to him.

other to...

QUIZ

People tease for lots of reasons—some nice, some not so nice. Sometimes you're just showing off your good sense of humour. Other times there's another goal, like bullying someone into something. This can cause harm. Read the following scenarios and decide whether they are examples of having humour or causing harm. Check your answers on the opposite page.

1 **Three Stooges**
Selim likes a girl in his class, and has confided in his friends Shawn and Sam. Shawn kids Selim a little about it when it's just the three of them. Sam, on the other hand, loudly jokes about it in front of the whole class.

2 **Bareheaded on the Bus**
A group of kids get on, talking and kidding around. One of them starts teasing a man because of his bald head. They all laugh.

3 **Spotted Sister**
Ryan teases his sister because she is the only one in the family that has freckles.

4 **Chubby Chum**
Max and Yasmina have an ongoing routine about how skinny one is, and how fat the other one is. The funniest thing is that they are both exactly the same size!

5 **Second-hand Rosa**
A popular girl teases a girl named Rosa because her clothes are always used or really lame store brands.

 Classmate Clowning
Conrad usually doesn't kid around much with his classmates, but he teases Mick because Mick is always teasing him.

 Hockey Holdup
Alecia teases her big brother about always being late to pick her up from hockey practice.

 Daddy Dearest
Carleen jokes around with her dad about how he stays at home and takes care of her, the way most people's moms do.

 The Pre-emptive Tease
Kalleigh spots Brit, the school's biggest practical joker, coming her way. Before Brit can say a word, Kalleigh starts loudly joking about Brit's big, fat behind.

 Favourite Enemies
Damon really, really doesn't like Darryl and makes fun of him all the time.

Answers

1. Harm. Shawn is making light of Selim's crush in a gentle way, but Sam runs of the risk of embarrassing Selim in front of the class—and the girl he likes.

2. Harm. Having a laugh like this at a stranger's expense is rude.

3. Humour. But if Ryan's teasing goes too far, it could make his sister feel like an outsider in her own family.

4. Humour. It sounds like these pals are both comfortable with the joke. It wouldn't be so funny, though, if one of them had issues with their body size.

5. Harm. Using this kind of humour to single out Rosa is mean and hurtful.

6. Humour. As long as no one's getting hurt, the teasing may just be their way of becoming pals.

7. Humour. This could be funny and may inspire Alecia's brother to be on time next time.

8. Humour. This is a shared joke. After all, there is nothing wrong with a dad staying at home.

9. Harm. If Kalleigh doesn't want to be teased, she should tell Brit to stop—not start a teasing war!

10. Harm. Whenever humour is used as a weapon against your enemies, it becomes bullying.

Dear Conflict Counsellor

Q. I'm trying to make friends in my new neighbourhood. Two guys on my street keep calling me "Porky" because I'm a little bit chunky. Their nicknames for each other, by the way, are "Banana Nose" and "Weasel." I don't mind nicknames, and these guys are fun, but how do I tell them that being called "Porky" hurts my feelings?
— *Th-th-that's All Folks*

A. Kids sometimes stick each other with awful nicknames. When everyone has one, it can be like belonging to a club. Judging by what the guys call each other, I'd guess they don't know they've hurt your feelings. If the nickname really bothers you, why not tell them? You could also suggest a name you find a whole lot funnier.

Q: One of the girls in our class turns red when she has to talk in class. The last time this happened, someone called her "Tomato" and she got really mad. She even cried! Everyone who laughed at the joke got in big-time trouble from the teacher. Man, some people have no sense of humour!

—*Just Kidding*

A: Sounds like you might be the one who needs to lighten up. How about giving this girl a break? How would you feel if someone pointed out something embarrassing about you in front of the class? Next time, try to put yourself in the other person's place. Ask yourself, "How would I feel if someone said that to me?" You might just stand up for that person instead of laughing.

Q: I am very tall for my age and I'm really tired of being teased about it. Every day, it's "How's the weather up there?" Even adults make these jokes. But here's what makes me really mad: I once called this short girl "Hobbit" and everyone told me it was totally rude. How come people can tease me but I can't tease back?

—*Tall, Not Tolerant*

A: Teasing people about their height—short or tall—can cause hurt feelings. Funny thing is, sometimes the teasing is meant as a compliment. In our society, being tall is considered a good thing, and people often assume no one minds being teased about a good thing. On the other hand, sometimes people make fun of others to feel better about themselves. In the end, it doesn't matter if people mean to hurt your feelings or not—they do. How about turning the teasing around? Next time, try saying something like, "We have a winner! That's the millionth time I've heard that old joke."

Q: The kid who sits in front of me in class keeps trying to get me in trouble with the teacher. He throws spit balls or even farts—and then blames me! All the other kids know it's him, but they go along with it because they think it is funny to see me get in trouble. Last time, the teacher threatened to send me to the principal for being rude.

—*Teasing Stinks*

A: It may be hard for the teacher to believe you when you're already in trouble, so find a quiet moment to explain the situation. Ask if you could be moved to another desk as far away as possible from your flatulent friend. That should clear the air.

Q: I have a great swimming coach, but he talks kind of weirdly. Some kids on the team do a killer imitation of him behind his back. I used to think it was hilarious, but yesterday the coach walked into the locker room while one of the boys was doing it. Coach laughed, but he had a funny look on his face. To be honest, I think it really upset him. Do you think a grown man could get that hurt by a stupid imitation?

—*Surprised Swimmer*

A: There is no age limit to having hurt feelings. Adults can be pretty good at hiding their emotions, so young people don't always realize when they've crossed the line. Think about it: if you've been teased all your life about something, it might get harder, not easier, to deal with over time. Time to tell your pals to quit doing the imitation, and maybe even apologize.

Myths

Why is everybody always picking on me?

Is it really that you're always being teased, or do you find it hard to take a joke? Sometimes the best protection from teasing is learning to laugh at yourself.

Girls are more sensitive than boys.

Some people are better at hiding their feelings than others. Boys are often told not to act too emotional, and so are adults. But that doesn't mean they don't hurt inside.

Teasers are bullies.

Yes, sometimes they are. But sometimes the reverse is true. Sometimes people tease others as a way of getting their attention because they like them.

DID YOU KNOW?

• In the Bible, some children teased a prophet named Elisha about his bald head. He sicced two bears on them!

It's not like I said something mean.

Teasing someone about something positive—like getting good marks or winning at sports—can be a roundabout way of giving a compliment. But it can still make the person feel uncomfortable or embarrassed.

It's okay for **adults** to tease **children** because they **know** when to **stop**.

Even adults have to be told if their teasing is hurtful.

Teasing is a **gentle** way to **offer** criticism.

If you think someone needs to hear your opinion, be straight and kind about it. Teasing might hurt their feelings. And if they think you're just joking, the message may not get through.

- When people are given puzzles to solve, they are called Brain Teasers. Rhymes that are hard to repeat are called Tongue Teasers.

- Lord Rochester asked King Charles II of England to knight his pet monkey. He was just teasing, of course!

You're such a joker.

That grinning guy in the Batman comics has nothing on you! You like to laugh and make other people laugh. Too bad some people have no sense of humour. Hey, that's their problem—you're just fooling around! It's not like you're hurting anyone. Or are you?

DEAR DR. SHRINK-WRAPPED . . .

NOW 10% DITZIER!

Blonde HAIR DYE

Q. I have an older brother who is quite a bit shorter than me. For as long as I can remember, I've called him nicknames like Shorty, Short-Stuff, Too Short, Mama's Little Shortening, and Short Shot. Yesterday, I called him "Short-Shorts" at breakfast and he got very angry and went screaming to his room. He hasn't spoken to me since. Why the short fuse all of a sudden? —*Long Face*

A. Hey, Long Face, ever hear about the straw that broke the camel's back? It refers to someone who kept adding stuff to a camel's load until suddenly the poor animal collapsed under the weight of one final, little straw. The same thing goes for your brother. He probably has never liked being called short, but he used to be able to ignore you. Yesterday, however, was the final straw. Dr. Shrink-Wrapped has two suggestions for you, if you want to make things right. First, apologize for all the short jokes in the past. And second, stop teasing him about his height from now on.

Q. Everybody likes me because I know a lot of jokes. Everybody, that is, except for this one girl who always freaks when I joke about dumb blondes. I know you shouldn't tell jokes about people because of their race or gender, but—heck!—I'm a blonde myself! If I want to make fun of myself to make other people laugh, I should be allowed to. What do you think?

—*Goldie-Locks*

A. Goldie, that's a type of humour known as a put-down. Putting others down makes some people feel better about themselves. Dr. Shrink-Wrapped has heard that blondes have more fun, so making jokes about them evens the score, right? Well … just like jokes about race or gender, jokes about blondes are based on **stereotypes**. A stereotype is the idea that people in a particular group share certain traits. Some stereotypes are positive, while others are negative. You might not mind these put-downs, but millions of other blondes may disagree with you. They might be tired of jokes that make them sound flaky, silly, or stupid.

YOU MUST BE SHORTER THAN THIS SIGN TO ENTER

QUIZ

Big Tease or Teasing Terror?

How do you know when your teasing isn't welcome? Take this quiz to find out how you rate on the teasing scale. Of the following statements, which ones are true about you and which ones false?

1 I often make remarks I think are funny at the time but later feel sorry I said them.

2 I seem to spend a lot of time saying, "Hey, I was only joking!"

3 When I call people funny names, they call me names back—often names that are not funny, but hurtful.

4 Some people seem to avoid me if they can help it.

5 Most of my jokes involve trying to make someone else feel bad or look stupid.

6 Often I seem to be the only one laughing.

7 I get told to "grow up" and "act your age" a lot.

8 I seem to have fewer friends than other people.

9 I tease people before they have a chance to say something bad about me.

10 I often get told to shut up.

11 I'm told to apologize a lot.

12 I am often mad at the people I tease.

13 Sometimes my friends "break up" with me.

14 My brother or sister complains about me to my parents.

15 I've been punished for teasing people.

16 My teacher mistakes my jokes for name-calling.

17 I have been left out of fun stuff because I was teasing someone.

18 I love pulling practical jokes, but my targets stop being my friends.

19 I have regretted teasing someone because they got mad at me.

20 I'm the only person I know with a really good sense of humour.

So, how did you do? Did you score a lot of trues? If so, you might try to think of better ways to make people laugh. Think about why you tease—is it to get noticed and be liked? How's that working out for you? Maybe you should talk to someone about how your teasing might be making both you and others unhappy.

How to stop hurting others

Most people who joke around just want to be liked and have fun. Who doesn't love the sound of laughter? Some people even make jokes for a living! Let's be real, though: any stand-up comedian will tell you that there's no perfect joke that makes everyone laugh. Fortunately, there are things you can do to ensure your friendly teasing never hurts your audience.

Think before you speak. Try to imagine how everyone around you will react if you say something funny. Do they all share your kind of humour?

Ask yourself, "How would I feel if someone said this to me?" If it sounds hurtful to you, it will probably be hurtful to someone else.

Check to see who else is listening. Even if you know the person you are teasing isn't offended, someone else in hearing range may be.

Pay attention to other people's comments. If they say your joking isn't funny, they're probably right. It is best not to tease them in the future.

Watch other people's expressions. Do they look embarrassed or unhappy when you tease them? Some people don't speak up when they are offended, but you may be upsetting them without knowing it.

DID YOU KNOW?

- Taco Bell once teased millions of people by announcing they had bought the famous Liberty Bell and were changing the name to the Taco Liberty Bell.

do's and don'ts

✓ Do consider other people's feelings.

✓ Do apologize immediately if you think you have accidentally hurt someone's feelings.

✓ Do pay attention to what you are actually saying.

✓ Do try to imagine in advance how people will react to your humour.

✓ Do learn the difference between gentle teasing and bullying.

✓ Do listen to how others make jokes and try to learn to be funny without being cruel.

✓ Do ask your friends if your teasing is unwelcome.

✓ Do tell people if you think their teasing is cruel.

✗ Don't dismiss negative feedback.

✗ Don't keep repeating the same teasing.

✗ Don't assume people have no sense of humour if they do not like your jokes.

✗ Don't blame the teased person for getting mad if he or she doesn't like your idea of what's funny.

✗ Don't make jokes about things about which you know people are sensitive.

✗ Don't tease people when you are angry.

✗ Don't tease back in the same offensive way when you are hurt by teasing.

Keep to yourself any comments you think might offend someone. It is best to not say something at all than to say something that might get you in trouble.

Go for quality, not quantity, in your jokes. People who make bad jokes all the time are annoying. At the end of the day, it is better to be remembered for one good joke than a dozen bad ones.

Be yourself. Sometimes people who tell jokes all the time are afraid that people won't like them unless they're funny. Your friends like you for your many good qualities, not just your sense of humour.

Try to find ways to make people laugh other than teasing them. Teasing is just one form of humour. You also can tell jokes, clown around, and even poke fun at yourself.

Canadian comedian Rick Mercer went to the United States and asked Americans to sign a petition to ban polar bear hunting in Toronto. Many did.

• St. Paul's real name was Saul. The name Paul is from the Latin word for "little." It is a teasing pun, or play on words, like calling him "Shorty."

It's not like you have no sense of humour.

You try to be a good sport, but for some reason other kids love to make you the butt of their jokes. When they do, you feel bullied and humiliated. You start sweating when someone is extra nice to you because you think it might be a set-up! And you're worried that if you stand up for yourself, it'll only make it worse.

do's and don'ts

✓ Do try to have a sense of humour.

✓ Do explain to a teaser why you are upset.

✓ Do tease back if you can do so in a non-offensive way.

✓ Do talk to your parents or a teacher if someone is making you unhappy with their teasing.

✓ Do try to think of a gentle comeback if you are always being teased with the same joke.

✓ Do try to make more friends, not just people who keep you around to be the butt of their jokes.

✗ Don't respond to cruelty by becoming cruel yourself.

✗ Don't think you are the only one being teased.

✗ Don't let someone get away with being offensive.

ninjaboy says:
Dude, that wasn't funny

✗ Don't hold a grudge if someone apologizes for having teased you.

✗ Don't lose your temper. That may be the reaction the teaser is looking for.

✗ Don't ignore your feelings.

✗ Don't be afraid to talk to someone you trust if the teasing becomes unbearable.

✗ Don't be shy about asking a friend to help you stand up to teasing and bullying.

QUIZ

Get some Face Time!

Getting teased all the time? There are basically three ways to respond to being picked-on repeatedly. You can get back at the teasers—be all In Your Face. Or, you can Hide Your Face and the hurt showing on it. Or you can Face Up to the person teasing you and show that they're not being so funny after all. Take this quiz and then check on the opposite page to see how you face teasing.

1 Punch-line Pals

You are still pretty new at your school, and you have been hanging with a guy who is always full of jokes. Trouble is, the jokes are always on or about you. Do you: a) Make cruel jokes back? b) Let him keep bugging you since he's your only friend right now? c) Ask him to stop, and if he doesn't, start looking for new friends?

2 Cool Shoes

A classmate keeps pointing out to everyone that your basketball shoes are way out of style. Do you: a) Tell your parents that you refuse to go to school until you get new shoes? b) Bounce a basketball off your classmate's face? Score! c) Tell your teaser that you have better things to do than to worry about staying in fashion?

3 Silly Sis

Your little sister keeps making fun of you because a guy in your class has asked you to a dance. Do you: a) Call her a buck-toothed weasel-faced little brat who will never get a boyfriend of her own? b) Tell your sister that the joke is getting bo-o-oring? c) Tell your parents and hope your sister gets in trouble?

4 Ball Blunder

In gym class, someone throws you a ball and you drop it. Some kid jokes, "Nice catch, Fumble-Fingers." Do you: a) Laugh it off and keep playing? b) Fake a sports injury to get out of the game? c) Run to the gym teacher and complain that someone called you a mean name?

5 Dare to Dance

You want to ask a girl out, but are afraid of being teased if your friends discover you like her. Do you: a) Ask her out in secret and hope your friends never find out? b) Ask her out and tell any teasers to grow up? c) Tell your friends that if they tease you, you'll tell the whole school that they were turned down by every girl in three grades?

6 Weighty Matters

There's a girl who is always making fun of your weight, even though she's bigger than you are! Do you: a) Point out in front of everyone how overweight she is? b) Ask her to quit making jokes about your weight because it hurts your feelings? c) Ignore her because it's pretty obvious that she's just trying to deflect negative attention from herself to you?

7 Sports Stars

Your coach is always making funny remarks to his best players, but never pals around with guys like you, the average players. Do you: a) Try to improve yourself at sports so that your coach will notice you, too? b) Politely point this habit out to the coach? c) Tease the coach that he has to favour his ace players, because his coaching isn't helping anyone else?

8 What's Your Beef?

You are a vegetarian. One kid in your class keeps joking that she is going to sneak a piece of meat into your lunch. Do you: a) Remind her that bulls, hippos, elephants may be vegetarians, but they are dangerous when they're angry? b) Start keeping a close eye on your lunch? c) Suggest she find out more about vegetarianism so she can understand why you do not eat meat?

9 Letting It Go to Your Head

A friend is always teasing you about your religious headdress. Do you: a) Tell her that you find her remarks offensive? b) Ignore her remarks and hope she will eventually get tired of teasing you? c) Loudly call her an ignorant racist?

10 Soccer Sniping

Your friend's dad is always teasing you about how his is son a better soccer player than you are. Do you: a) Tell him that his son is lousy at other stuff, like schoolwork? B) Not say anything because he is your friend's dad? c) Tell him calmly—or ask your friend to tell him—that his comments aren't appreciated?

Answers

1. a) In Your Face
   b) Hide Your Face
   c) Face Up

2. a) Hide Your Face
   b) In Your Face
   c) Face Up

3. a) In Your Face
   b) Face Up
   c) Hide Your Face

4. a) Face Up
   b) Hide Your Face
   c) In Your Face

5. a) Hide Your Face
   b) Face Up
   c) In Your Face

6. a) In Your Face
   b) Face Up
   c) Hide Your Face

7. a) Hide Your Face
   b) Face Up
   c) In Your Face

8. a) In Your Face
   b) Hide Your Face
   c) Face Up

9. a) Face Up
   b) Hide Your Face
   c) In Your Face

10. a) In Your Face
    b) Hide Your Face
    c) Face Up

Time to terminate the teasing.

There are some basic things you can do when you are tired of being picked-on.

Keep Your Cool.
People tease to get a response. If there is no reaction, they will often give up. Try ignoring your teaser if you can.

Be Prepared.
Some people constantly repeat themselves when they tease. Try to think of a good comeback. For example, if they are always making fun of your name, say something like "Gee, I haven't heard that one since kindergarten," or "Better check your head, Fred, you seem to be stuck on Repeat."

Gently Challenge.
Some teasers do not realize that they are being annoying. Sometimes, if you just tell them that you do not like being teased, they will apologize and back off.

Show Determination.
If you politely ask to not be teased and it still continues, tell your teaser that you will ask your teacher or parents to step in if you have to.

DID YOU KNOW?

- Every year, a bar holds a Bad Hemingway contest, in which contestants try to compose pieces like Ernest Hemingway's worst writing.

When political correctness is involved

You may have heard about political correctness. Being politically correct means to avoid saying things that will insult or exclude people. It is one way to fight stereotypes—set ideas about particular groups of people. Making jokes about certain subjects tends to be politically incorrect. Those subjects include:

- race
- religion
- profession
- gender (whether someone is male or female)
- physical traits or disabilities

Some people think it is their right to say whatever they want, whenever they please. Others think that no one should ever make jokes that may offend anyone, anywhere, at any time. Neither side is absolutely right.

If you are always politically *incorrect*, there's no doubt you will upset a lot of people. If you are always politically *correct*, you might find it difficult to deal with people who don't meet your high standards, and you'll definitely miss out on some humour. If you like jokes but also want friends, you have to find the middle ground where you can make and hear jokes but don't offend people. The trouble is, the middle ground keeps changing!

Have you ever heard people from a certain group make a joke about themselves? They all laughed, right? What happens when someone from outside that group makes the same joke? Not funny, is it? And why? Well, within the group, people are finding humour in something they have *in common*. When someone outside the group makes the same joke, they are poking fun at that group's *differences* from everyone else.

If someone ever tells you that you've crossed the line, try to respect that person's views and apologize. Remember, it's not up to you to decide what others find funny.

The Final Straw.
If the teasing continues even after you have asked not to be teased, and you have warned that you will get an adult involved, then ask your teacher or parents for help in dealing with the situation.

Boxer Muhammad Ali teased his opponents in the ring to make them lose their tempers and make mistakes.

- Motorcycle racer Valentino Rossi often teased his opponents by letting them pass and then zooming into the lead again.

There's nothing better than a belly laugh.

You like to make jokes, hear jokes, and even be the target of jokes. Not much gets to you. But not everyone can roll with the punches like you do. Every day you see someone getting hurt or causing hurt by teasing.

Too bad you can't say anything.
Or can you?

Should you?

Part of the Problem

There is an old legal saying in Latin: *Qui tacet consentit*. This means "silence implies consent." In other words, if you don't speak up when you see others doing wrong, it suggests you're going along with it.

People are often surprised to find out how much their opinion means to their friends. Next time you see a buddy hurting someone by teasing, don't laugh—there's a good chance your friend will stop. Or try speaking up. This can be hard to do, but not standing up for your beliefs makes you part of the problem. Will you lose your friend over it? If your friendship is strong, it'll survive.

Humour is Hard

Humour can be a difficult thing to share, understand, or even explain for a number of reasons.

- We all like to laugh, but a joke can make one person laugh and another person feel hurt or unhappy.
- The rules can change from person to person and situation to situation.
- People like to laugh—and sometimes even to be teased—but they do not like to be attacked with insults or abuse.

One general rule to remember is that if a joke embarrasses anyone, then it is not okay. If you want to learn how to make people laugh, listen to someone who can do it well without hurting other people's feelings. With a little practice, you might become a funnier person, too.

do's and don'ts

✓ Do laugh if a joke is harmless and funny.

✓ Do ask a teaser to listen if someone asks him or her to stop teasing.

✓ Do report hurtful remarks to your teachers or parents if you do not feel comfortable confronting the teaser yourself.

✓ Do ask your teacher to have a class discussion about why some jokes are funny and others are not.

✓ Do try to help a friend apologize if he or she has hurt someone's feelings.

✓ Do support someone who has been teased.

✗ Don't join your friends in making hurtful jokes or remarks.

✗ Don't assume that teasing doesn't bother someone just because they do not appear angry.

✗ Don't be afraid that you will lose a friend if you don't laugh.

✗ Don't let a friend continue teasing someone if you know it is harmful.

✗ Don't assume that someone who is upset about being teased is overly sensitive.

✗ Don't encourage anyone to make racist, sexist, or hateful remarks.

✗ Don't be surprised if a joker didn't realize that his or her teasing has been hurtful.

✗ Don't distance yourself from someone being teased.

QUIZ

Do you really get it?

It's hard to know what to do when teasing gets out of hand. But you do have choices! What would you do in the following situations? This quiz has no right or wrong answers, because each situation—and every person—is different. Your answers might be different from the ones suggested here, but they could be right under the circumstances.

1 THE TEASE MONSTER

Dwayne is a bully. He is always teasing other kids, and you are afraid that, if you don't laugh along with his teasing, he might start picking on you too.

- Ignore Dwayne. If he doesn't get a reaction, he might stop.
- Stand up for the kids that Dwayne teases.
- If someone is really getting hurt, let an adult know what's going on.

2 TWO MOMS

One of kids at your school has two mothers but no father. Your friends have started teasing the kid about his mothers being gay.

- Point out to your friends that their jokes about the mothers' sexual orientation may be really offensive to some people, especially the kid.
- Let the kid know that not everyone feels the same way as your friends.
- Talk to a counsellor or teacher about workshops on tolerance and sexual orientation.

3 Race Riot

A friend of yours is always telling racist jokes that he thinks are hilarious. He thinks it is all right so long as no one from another race can hear him.

- Never laugh at any of your friend's racist jokes.
- Tell your friend that his jokes make you uncomfortable.
- If he won't stop, and his jokes continue to make you uncomfortable, consider making new friends.

4 ALL IN THE FAMILY

Your older sister loves cruelly teasing your little brother. They always end up in a big fight, and then your parents punish all of you.

- Ask your sister to stop teasing your brother.
- Help your brother stand up to your sister.
- Consult with your parents about the fairness of punishing all of you.

5 The Butt of the Joke

There is a new kid in your class whose last name is Butt. Everyone is teasing him.

- Try to make friends with the new kid.
- Find out if the teasing is bothering the new kid.
- Point out to your friends that it would be awfully hard to be teased so much on top of being at a new school.

6 THE DAILY "SPECIAL"

Every day, a bus brings a group of Special Ed kids to school. Everybody makes comments about the kids on that bus, and your friends have started to tease the kids to their faces.

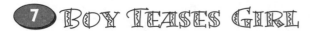

- Stand up for the kids on the bus, and explain why the teasing bothers you.
- Point out to your friends that Special Ed can mean a lot of different things.
- Don't join in or laugh when your friends tease the kids.

7 BOY TEASES GIRL

Because your best friend Dal likes a girl named Kerry, he keeps teasing her to get her attention. Unfortunately, the constant teasing is turning off Kerry, and she is starting to show interest in you instead.

- Tell Kerry that you can't return her interest without hurting Dal.
- Help Dal think of better ways to get Kerry's attention.
- Point out to Dal that his plan is backfiring.

8 *Toon Teasing*

You and your friends are watching an old cartoon and it is full of dumb jokes about women.

- Do a research project on the era when the cartoon was made, and the events that have happened since then in women's rights.
- Talk with your friends about why you find the outdated humour funny or offensive and how ideas about women have changed over time.
- Offer to turn off the cartoon if anyone finds it offensive.

DID YOU KNOW?

- When the first stuffed platypus arrived from Australia, British scientists were convinced the animal was a hoax.

⑨ Put It Down in Black and White

Two of your friends are African Canadian, and they are always making jokes to each other about things their families have in common. When a white kid made a similar joke, your friends got really mad.

- Tell your friends to explain to the kid why they were so offended by his joke.
- Stop making or laughing at jokes about stereotypes of any kind if you do not want to have to keep explaining why some are funny and some are not.

⑩ TOUCHY ABOUT TEASING

A kid in your class is very sensitive and breaks into tears every time anyone says anything negative to her. You know she hates how easily she cries.

- Talk to your friends and agree that you will all lay off this girl.
- Point out to the girl that just because people tease her doesn't mean she isn't likable.
- Discuss with the girl ways she could calm herself down when she starts getting upset. She could count to ten, for instance, or ask people to stop teasing her before it goes too far.

- In 1938, actor Orson Welles panicked millions of Americans with a radio program that reported that Martians were invading the Earth.

- Before First Nations warriors fought each other in battle, they used to hurl insults and verbally tease their enemies, sometimes for hours.

More **Help**

It takes time and practice to learn the skills in this book. There are many ways to deal with teasing, but only you know what feels right for you in different situations. In the end, the best response is the one that doesn't hurt anyone's feelings.

If you need more information or someone to talk to, these resources might help.

Helplines

Kids Help Phone (Canada) 1-800-668-6868
Youth Crisis Hotline (USA) 1-800-448-4663

Web sites

Canadian Safe Schools Network: www.cssn.org
Kids Help Phone: www.kidshelp.sympatico.ca

Books

The Black Sunshine of Goody Pryne by Sarah Withrow, Groundwood Books, 2003.
The Bully: A Discussion and Activity Story, by Rita Toews, Birds Hill Publishing, 2004.
Frog Face and the Three Boys by Don Tremblath, Orca Book Publishers, 2000
The Joke's on Us by Gordon Korman, Scholastic, 2004.
Maxx Comedy by Gordon Korman, Scholastic, 2003.
My Name is Mitch by Shelagh Lynne Supeene, Orca Book Publishers, 2003.
No More Pranks by Monique Polak, Orca Book Publishers, 2004.
The Prank by K.E. Calder, Vanwell Publishing, 2003.
So Long Stinky Queen by Frieda Wishinsky, Fitzhenry and Whiteside, 2000.
Zee's Way by Kristin Butcher, Orca Book Publishers, 2004.

Other titles in the Deal With It series:

Arguing: Deal with it word by word by Elaine Slavens, illustrated by Steven Murray.
Authority: Deal with it before it deals with you by Anne Marie Aikins, illustrated by Steven Murray.
Bullying: Deal with it before push comes to shove by Elaine Slavens, illustrated by Brooke Kerrigan.
Competition: Deal with it from start to finish by Mireille Messier, illustrated by Steven Murray.
Fighting: Deal with it without coming to blows by Elaine Slavens, illustrated by Steven Murray.
Girlness: Deal with it body and soul by Diane Peters, illustrated by Steven Murray.
Gossip: Deal with it before word gets around by Catherine Rondina, illustrated by Dan Workman.
Guyness: Deal with it body and soul by Steve Pitt, illustrated by Steven Murray.
Misconduct: Deal with it without bending the rules by Anne Marie Aikins, illustrated by Steven Murray.
Peer Pressure: Deal with it without losing your cool by Elaine Slavens, illustrated by Ben Shannon.
Privacy: Deal with it like nobody's business by Diane Peters, illustrated by Jeremy Tankard.
Procrastination: Deal with it all in good time by Diane Peters, illustrated by Jeremy Tankard.
Racism: Deal with it before it gets under your skin by Anne Marie Aikins, illustrated by Steven Murray.
Rudeness: Deal with it if you please by Catherine Rondina, illustrated by Dan Workman.

Text copyright © 2010 by Steve Pitt
Illustrations copyright © 2010 by Remie Geoffroi

All rights reserved. No part of this book may be reproduced or transmitted in any form or by any means, electronic or mechanical, including photocopying, or by any information storage or retrieval system, without permission in writing from the Publisher.

James Lorimer & Company Ltd. acknowledges the support of the Ontario Arts Council. We acknowledge the financial support of the Government of Canada through the Canada Book Fund for our publishing activities. We acknowledge the support of the Canada Council for the Arts for our publishing program. We acknowledge the support of the Government of Ontario through the Ontario Media Development Corporation's Ontario Book Initiative.

The Canada Council for the Arts | Le Conseil des Arts du Canada

ONTARIO ARTS COUNCIL
CONSEIL DES ARTS DE L'ONTARIO

Series design: Blair Kerrigan/Glyphics

Library and Archives Canada Cataloguing in Publication

Pitt, Steve, 1954-
    Teasing : deal with it before the joke's on you / Steve Pitt ; illustrated by Remie Geoffroi.

(Deal with it)
ISBN 978-1-55277-497-7 (bound)
ISBN 978-1-55028-946-6 (pbk.)

III. Series: Deal with it (Toronto, Ont.)

BF637.T43P58 2010   j302.3   C2010-900280-6

James Lorimer & Company Ltd., Publishers
317 Adelaide Street West, Suite #1002
Toronto, Ontario
M5V 1P9
www.lorimer.ca

Printed in China, bound in Canada